THE GREAT BOOK OF SCOTLA

AN EDUCATIONAL COUNTRY TRAVEL PICTURE BOOK FOR KIDS ABOUT HISTORY, DESTINATION PLACES, ANIMALS AND MANY MORE

Copyright @2023 James K. Mahi

All rights reserved

Scotland is part of the United Kingdom and located in the northern part of Great Britain.

The official language spoken in Scotland is English, but there's also a unique Scottish Gaelic language.

Scotland is famous for its beautiful castles, like Edinburgh Castle and Eilean Donan Castle.

Scotland has over 790 islands, including the Orkney Islands, the Shetland Islands, and the Hebrides.

The Scottish flag is called the Saltire, which is a white X-shaped cross on a blue background.

The capital city of Scotland is **Edinburgh**.

The national animal of Scotland is the **unicorn**.

Scotland has stunning landscapes, including mountains, valleys, and rugged coastline.

The highest mountain in Scotland is **Ben Nevis**, which stands at 1,345 meters (4,413 feet).

DISCLAIMER: ⚠
SCOTCH WHISKY IS AN ALCOHOLIC DRINK AND SHOULD NOT BE CONSUMED BY CHILDREN. THIS BOOK IS FOR INFORMATIONAL PURPOSES ONLY AND DOES NOT PROMOTE THE CONSUMPTION OF ALCOHOL BY MINORS.

Scotch whisky, also known as Scotch, is a **famous alcoholic drink made in Scotland.**

Scotland's national dish is **haggis**, a savory dish made from sheep's heart, liver, and lungs, mixed with oats and spices, cooked in a sheep's stomach.

The sport of **golf was invented in Scotland**, and it has many world-renowned golf courses.

The Scottish people celebrate their heritage and culture during events called Highland Games, where you can watch sports like caber tossing and hammer throwing.

Edinburgh hosts the **world's largest arts festival** called the Edinburgh Festival Fringe, where performers from all over the world showcase their talents.

Scotland is home to many famous inventors and engineers, such as **Alexander Graham Bell and James Watt.**

The official flower of Scotland is the thistle, a prickly purple plant.

The Isle of Skye is a picturesque island in Scotland known for its rugged landscapes and fairy-tale-like scenery.

The Kelpies are massive horse-head sculptures near Falkirk, representing the country's strong ties to horses.

The Forth Bridge in Scotland is an iconic engineering marvel and a UNESCO World Heritage Site.

St. Andrew's Day on November 30th is the national day of Scotland, honoring its patron saint, Saint Andrew.

Scotland has a rich history, including ancient clans and battles like the Battle of Culloden.

The Shetland Islands in Scotland are known for their adorable Shetland ponies.

The Scottish Highlands are known for their breathtaking beauty and stunning scenery.

The official sport of Scotland is shinty, a team sport similar to field hockey.

The River Tay is the longest river in Scotland.

The famous author Sir Walter Scott wrote many novels inspired by Scotland, such as "Ivanhoe" and "Rob Roy."

Scotland's landscapes have been featured in popular movies like "Braveheart" and "Harry Potter."

The Isle of Arran is often called "Scotland in Miniature" because it has a bit of everything the country has to offer.

The national bird of Scotland is the golden eagle.

The Hebrides are a group of islands off the west coast of Scotland known for their stunning beaches and wildlife.

Scotland has over 790 offshore islands.

The Edinburgh Zoo is home to the UK's only giant pandas, Tian Tian and Yang Guang.

Edinburgh is known for its annual Hogmanay celebrations, one of the world's biggest New Year's Eve parties.

The Scottish people have their own traditional clothing called the kilt, usually worn by men.

The Caledonian Canal, which connects the east and west coasts of Scotland, has a series of locks and is a popular spot for boating.

The fairy pools on the Isle of Skye are natural pools with crystal-clear blue water.

The Scottish Parliament, located in Edinburgh, makes decisions on matters that affect Scotland.

Inverness is often referred to as the "Gateway to the Highlands."

The Edinburgh Castle is built on an ancient volcanic rock called Castle Rock.

The town of Falkirk is home to the Falkirk Wheel, the world's only rotating boat lift.

The Isle of Lewis in Scotland has ancient standing stones called the Callanish Stones.

The West Highland Way is a famous long-distance hiking trail that takes you through some of Scotland's most scenic landscapes.

The national instrument of Scotland is the bagpipes.

The Royal Mile in Edinburgh is a historic street lined with shops, pubs, and street performers.

The Firth of Forth is an estuary where you can see the famous Forth Rail Bridge.

Scotland's rich history, stunning nature, and friendly people make it a fantastic destination for tourists of all ages.

TOP 15 TRAVEL TIPS FOR VISITING SCOTLAND

1. **Pack Warm Clothes:** Scotland can be chilly, even in summer. Bring sweaters, jackets, and rainproof gear.
2. **Rainy Days Prepared:** Carry an umbrella or waterproof jacket to stay dry during occasional rain showers.
3. **Currency:** Use British Pounds (GBP) for shopping and payments.
4. **Public Transport:** Buses and trains are great for exploring cities and countryside. Get an Explorer Pass for discounts.
5. **Driving Rules:** If you're driving, remember to stay on the left side of the road. Follow the speed limits.
6. **Cash and Cards:** Many places accept credit and debit cards, but it's good to have some cash for small purchases.
7. **Emergency Number:** Remember 999 for emergencies like accidents or medical help.
8. **Tipping:** Tipping isn't always necessary, but it's polite to leave a small tip in restaurants and for good service.
9. **Local Etiquette:** Scots are friendly, so saying "please" and "thank you" is appreciated.
10. **Free Attractions:** Visit free attractions like museums and parks to save money.
11. **Electricity**: The voltage is 230V, so bring a plug adapter if your devices have different plugs.
12. **Local Food:** Try traditional Scottish dishes like haggis, neeps, and tatties for a taste of the culture.
13. **Language:** English is widely spoken, but you might hear Scottish Gaelic too.
14. **Stay Safe:** Follow signs and guidelines, especially when exploring nature or hiking.
15. **Enjoy Nature:** Scotland's landscapes are stunning. Explore castles, lochs, and highlands for unforgettable views.

TOP 15 TRAVEL PLACES IN SCOTLAND

1. **Edinburgh**: The capital city with a castle on a hill, old streets, and a famous festival called the Edinburgh Festival.
2. **Glasgow**: A lively city with art, music, and museums. It's friendly and known for its good shopping.
3. **Loch Ness**: A big, mysterious lake where people look for a legendary monster called Nessie.
4. **The Highlands**: Beautiful mountains and valleys where you can hike and see incredible landscapes.
5. **Isle of Skye**: An island with stunning views, rocky landscapes, and charming villages.
6. **St. Andrews**: A historic town with a famous golf course and an old university.
7. **Inverness**: A city near Loch Ness, surrounded by history and Highland culture.
8. **Stirling**: A place with a cool castle and stories about famous people from Scotland's past.
9. **Aberdeen**: A coastal city with nice parks, a sandy beach, and a lively port.
10. **Scottish Borders**: A quiet place with pretty countryside, historic houses, and the lovely River Tweed.
11. **Dundee**: A city by the sea with interesting museums, a cool science center, and a tall ship you can explore.
12. **Oban**: A cozy town on the west coast, famous for seafood, ferries to islands, and beautiful sunsets.
13. **Fort William**: Near the tallest mountain in the UK, Ben Nevis, it's great for hiking and outdoor adventures.
14. **Orkney Islands**: A group of islands with ancient ruins, stunning cliffs, and a unique culture.
15. **Edinburgh Zoo**: A fun place to see animals, including pandas, and learn about wildlife conservation.

Printed in Great Britain
by Amazon